Look What We've Brought You From
KOREA

Crafts, Games, Recipes, Stories, and Other Cultural Activities

From Korean Americans

Phyllis Shalant
Illustrated by Soyoo Hyunjoo Park

JULIAN ⊗ MESSNER

Published by Julian Messner, a division of Silver Burdett Press, Inc., 250 James Street, Morristown, NJ 07960.

JULIAN MESSNER and colophon are trademarks of Simon & Schuster.

Book design by Anahid Hamparian

10 9 8 7 6 5 4 3 2 1

Library of Congress Cataloging-in Publication Data

Shalant, Phyllis.
    Look what we've brought you from Korea: crafts, games, recipes, stories, and other cultural activities
from Korean Americans / by Phyllis Shalant ; [illustrations by Soyoo Hyunjoo Park].
        p.   cm.
    Includes bibliographical references.
    1. Korea—Social life and customs—Juvenile literature. [1. Korea—Social life and customs.]   I. Park,
    Soyoo Hyunjoo, ill.   II. Title.
    DS904.S457   1994   951.9—dc20
    ISBN 0-671-88701-7 (hardcover)   94-25829
    ISBN 0-671-88702-5 (paperback)   CIP
                                                       AC

ACKNOWLEDGMENTS

MANY PEOPLE contributed their time and knowledge to the writing of this book. The Korean Cultural Service in New York City provided access to its wonderful library of books and videos, and its librarian, Sook Kih Park, was most generous with her help. Mr. and Mrs. Kwon of Ardsley, New York, taught me to play yoot and to make a jaegi. Soyoo Hyunjoo Park, the illustrator of this book and an artist and teacher who directs the Korean cultural program at Camp Sejong in Demarest, New Jersey, graciously offered many suggestions. Sung-Joo Park, Youth Minister of the Korean Presbyterian Church in Tarrytown, New York, took time out on a busy morning to be of assistance. Bok-Soon Schwartz helped test the recipes. Herb Shalant provided expert technical assistance in adapting the crafts activities. As always, Mary Slamin and Mary Burnap found every Korean folktale in the Westchester Library System. My sincere thanks to all!

CONTENTS

INTRODUCTION

*T*HE TIGER is the best known symbol of Korea. For centuries, this proud creature has been used to represent the strength and character of the Korean people in folk tales, arts, and crafts. All over Korea, the tiger can be seen decorating everything from buildings to clothing.

Located precariously between China and Japan, Korea has always needed the strength and bravery of a tiger to keep from being overtaken by its more powerful neighbors. Yet, although the three nations share many common traits, Korean culture has managed to keep its own unique characteristics. Sadly, though, in 1945, this land that had been united for 1,000 years was broken into two countries. These independent countries, which are commonly referred to as South Korea and North Korea, continue to exist as separate nations today.

In the past ten years, more than 300,000 South Koreans have come to the United States. Perhaps you have eaten in a Korean restaurant, shopped in a Korean market, or met a Korean-American student in your school. If so, you already know that you're in for a treat! The Korean culture is full of fun, from its lively games to its hot and spicy food.

The flag of the Republic of Korea (the formal name of South Korea) contains many symbols. In the center of a white field is a circle with a red and blue swirl. The contrasting colors symbolize the universe in perfect harmony and balance. The sets of bars at each corner of the flag stand for ideas of opposites and balance. The three unbroken bars symbolize heaven; the three broken bars symbolize earth. The bars in the lower left symbolize fire; the bars in the upper right symbolize water.

KOREA—"OVER THE MOUNTAINS, MORE MOUNTAINS"

Both North and South Korea are located on the 600-mile long Korean peninsula, which extends from China into the Sea of Japan. The entire peninsula covers an area of 85,049 square miles, which is about the same size as Utah. In addition, there are more than 3,000 islands that lie off the southern and western coasts.

Koreans have many sayings about their land. One of these, san nomo san itta, means "over the mountains, more mountains." If you ever visit Korea, you will see why. Beautiful mountains border the horizon almost everywhere you look. Mount Paektu is the highest peak at 9,003 feet.

Seoul is the capital of South Korea and its largest city. The capital of North Korea, Pyongyang, is also its largest city. Since the governments of the two countries are enemies, relatives living in one country are unable to visit those in the other. Some family members have been separated for fifty years. This is particularly tragic for Koreans because they value family above all else.

HOLIDAY FUN

Sul, New Year's Day

SOME KOREANS, especially those who live in cities, celebrate the New Year on January 1, just as we do in the West. Many Korean families, however, choose to celebrate the traditional lunar New Year, Sul, which falls on the first day of the first lunar month, usually late in January or early in February. (The lunar calendar system is based on the moon and was introduced to Korea from China.) Whichever New Year they choose to observe, the celebrations are almost the same.

Like most Korean holidays, this day is centered around the family. The morning begins with ceremonies to remember ancestors. All over the land, people eat a special rice cake soup known as ttokkuk. To make the "cakes" for this soup, steamed, sticky rice is pounded into a stick shape and then cut into pieces shaped like coins. The pieces are mixed with water, meat, soy sauce, sesame oil, scallions, and an egg. These ingredients are combined at various stages to make this special soup. Tradition says that a bowl of this soup eaten on New Year's Day makes you one year older. Koreans like to joke that if you eat four bowls, you'll be four years older!

On New Year's Day, many people often dress in the hanbok. Men wear the paji chogori, traditional baggy pants and shirts. Women and girls wear the chima chogon, a long, full skirt and shirt made of light, colorful silk. Older family members remain at home and wait to be visited by their children and grandchildren, who perform a special bowing ceremony called sebae. In return the elders give the children spending money to put in their special good-luck purses. Then the games begin! Adults and youngsters test their skills in kite-flying contests, often with homemade kites. Girls play a traditional game of jumping on see-saws. And everyone, young and old, plays Korea's most popular board game. To try your luck at yoot, see page 30.

MAKE A KITE FOR SUL

TRADITIONAL KOREAN kites are easy to make. The most common is shaped like a rectangle and has a hole cut out in its center. On New Year's Day, kite-flying contests are held everywhere. Participants apply paste to the strings of their kites and rub glass powder into the glue to make the strings sharp. Then as their kites soar in the sky, the fliers cross their strings and "fight" until, one by one, the string of each opponent's kite is cut and the kite flies away. The last kite left flying in the sky is the winner.

Follow the instructions below to make your own high flier.

MATERIALS:

- a rectangular sheet of rice paper approximately 17" x 24" (Rice paper is available in many art supply stores, but you may substitute another light, strong paper, if necessary.)
- white wood glue
- 6 sticks, approximately 30" each, made of bamboo, balsa, or spruce wood (The sticks should be at least as long as the diagonal length of the kite.)
- kite string
- scissors, heavy enough to cut your sticks
- cotton swab
- pencil
- 2 lb. coffee can (empty) or other cylindrical container that has a 5" diameter

INSTRUCTIONS:

1. Fold the rice paper in quarters. Open and place the coffee can in the center where the fold lines cross. Trace around the can with a pencil. Now cut out the circle.

2. Using one of the sticks as a ruler, lightly draw a diagonal line across the paper from corner to corner. Repeat across other two corners so you have drawn an "X". Now draw a straight line across the width of the paper, about 1/2" from the top edge. Repeat across bottom.

3. Using the scissors, cut three sticks at least 1" longer than the width of the paper, one stick at least 1" longer than the length of the paper, and two sticks

at least 1" longer than the two diagonal lines you have drawn.

4. Apply a very thin bead of glue along the fold lines and the diagonals you have drawn, excluding a 2" area where the sticks are going to overlap. (Not putting glue on the paper where the sticks overlap will make it easier to tie the overlap with string later on.)

5. Lay the sticks on top of the glue lines in this order: a) top edge horizontal; b) bottom edge horizontal; c) horizontal across middle; d) diagonal; e) diagonal; f) vertical across middle. Four of the sticks will overlap in the middle of the cutout hole. Lightly press the sticks down into the glue.

6. Wait about three minutes after all the sticks have been placed on the paper and are sticking to it. Now turn the kite over. This will allow the paper to stay in contact with all the sticks without letting it stick to the table or work surface. Let the glue dry overnight.

7. When the kite is dry, tie all the overlapped sticks together with several twists of kite string and knot tightly. At this time, the sticks can be trimmed to extend about 1/2" beyond the paper.

8. Dip cotton swab in glue and apply sparingly to the paper under the sticks in the areas you avoided gluing previously. Allow to dry.

9. Decorate your kite. Traditional Korean designs include the red-and-blue swirl and multicolored bands.

10. To make the kite more aerodynamic, bow it as shown in the diagram. You will have to make a small hole in the paper about 4" from the bottom. Reinforce the area around the hole with a patch of leftover rice paper (you can use this method to repair kite tears as well). Attach your kite-flying string and catch a breeze!

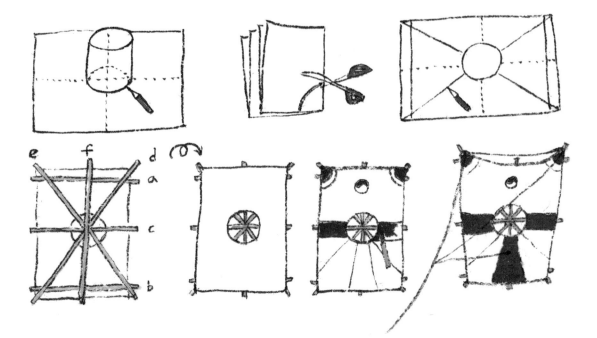

Dano, the Spring Festival

DANO HONORS new growth and spring rain. It is celebrated on the fifth day of the fifth month of the lunar calendar, the time between the planting of rice seedlings and their transfer to the paddy fields. On this joyous spring holiday, the Korean people spend much time in outdoor amusements. The best known of these activities is swinging. Thin, strong tree trunks or poles are used to create a tall frame that is connected at the top with a cross beam. Thick ropes for the swing are hung from the beam, and are then connected to a plank seat. Or else a single rope may be hung in a "U" shape for the swinger to stand on. The structure may be twenty feet high!

Although boys may build the swing's frame, the swinging is usually done by girls. They stand while they fly through the air, letting their colorful hanboks flap like butterfly wings. Sometimes a contest is held to see who can swing the highest. Koreans say that if a girl swings high enough once, her toes will reach heaven. If she swings high enough twice, her dreams will reach the heavens.

Other activities at Dano include ssireum, a kind of folk wrestling that is considered a national sport. In ssireum, two opponents begin by facing each other kneeling down and holding onto each other. Each contestant's right hand holds his opponent's waist band, while his left hand holds the other's right leg. At the signal to start, they stand up together and begin wrestling. The one whose body or hand touches the ground first is the loser.

Koreans are a people close to nature. At Dano, it was a custom of village girls to collect iris roots and leaves that they boiled in water to make a hair rinse. This rinse, which is said to add health and vitality to the hair and body, represents the promise of spring.

Seesawing, Korean Style

AT DANO, girls also like to play the folk sport of seesaw bouncing, which is said to have originated during ancient times when girls over the age of seven were forbidden to leave their high-walled yards. To see over the walls, girls developed their seesaw play into an acrobatic skill. Today, of course, the game is played for fun. Each player tries to jump as hard and as high as possible, while keeping up a steady rhythm.

It's not as easy as it sounds! Players need good balance and a soft spot to land in case they fall. If you decide to try this game, be sure to play it only outside on a grassy lawn, or on a large padded mat in your school gym.

HOW TO MAKE A KOREAN SEESAW:

MATERIALS:
- wooden board, about 7 feet x 1 1/2 feet
- a bundle of straw, a rolled mat or sleeping bag, or a large cushion for pivot
- two or three players

TO PLAY:

A soft, grass-covered lawn is the best place for this game. To create the seesaw, just place the straw bundle or rolled mat under the middle of the board. First, the "center person" crouches down in the middle of the board, using a hand on each side to balance herself. Now a player stands on each end and alternates jumping to propel the player on the opposite side as high as she can. In turn, when that player lands back on the board, she launches her companion.

The first person to break the rhythm—or to fall off the board—changes places with the center person.

TAK SSAUM, A BALANCING-WRESTLING GAME

ALTHOUGH KOREA has a prospering economy today, it was for a long time a poor country. Toys were homemade and youngsters created their own games. One game is a kind of version of traditional Korean wrestling called tak ssaum. Playing tak ssaum, which means "cock-fighting," requires balance, strength, and quickness.

HOW TO PLAY:

Tak ssaum must only be played on a grassy lawn or on a gym mat.

This game requires two people to play—and others to cheer. Each opponent begins by standing on one leg and bending the other leg in front, so he can hold onto the foot of that leg in his opposite hand. At the starting signal, the contestants begin to bump against each other—until someone falls. The person left standing is the winner, who may now face another opponent.

이겨라! 이겨라!

CH'USOK, THE KOREAN THANKSGIVING

CH'USOK MEANS harvest or full moon. Ch'usok is also called Pal Wall Hangawi. It is celebrated on the fifteenth day of the eighth lunar month, which usually falls in September or October. Ch'usok is a day when Koreans give thanks for a rich harvest, just as Americans do on Thanksgiving. Like Thanksgiving, it is celebrated with much feasting. Preparations begin days before the holiday. Newly harvested grain is used to make special rice cakes called songpyon. The cakes are made in a half-moon shape and filled with sweet soy bean paste or sesame seed paste.

The family-oriented Koreans never forget their ancestors. On Ch'usok, as on all holidays, ceremonies honoring the dead are held. Songpyon is taken to family tombs as a symbolic offering with other foods. Afterward, young people play traditional outdoor games. In times past, it was the custom for rural folk to climb the hilltops on Ch'usok night. There they would swing lighted torches in circles to greet the harvest moon.

Kimchi, A Special Dish

In late autumn, after Ch'usok, Koreans start to prepare foods for the winter. One of the most important foods is kimchi. This spicy, pickled vegetable dish can be found at every Korean meal. The most common types of kimchi are made with cabbage, cucumber, turnips, or radishes, although other vegetables can be substituted. Fruit and even seafood may be prepared this way as well. In fact, Koreans say there are about 200 different varieties of kimchi! But the ingredients always include red pepper, garlic, scallions, ginger root, and salt.

Kimchi is traditionally stored in special pots called kim jahng dak. All over Korea, these dark brown earthenware jars are stored under the ground or in a cool basement or on a deck or terrace of an apartment.

Kimchi dishes range from mildly spicy to very hot, so it's a good idea to eat them with plenty of white rice alongside.

HOW TO MAKE CABBAGE KIMCHI:

INGREDIENTS:

- 5 cups of cabbage cut into bite-size pieces.
  (If you can find Korean Napa cabbage, use this, but any variety will do.)
- 6 tablespoons of salt
- 2 tablespoons of sugar
- 2 teaspoons to 2 tablespoons of crushed red pepper
  flakes, the kind you usually put on pizza. (Be very careful.
  Red pepper flakes are hot, so if you are not accustomed to
  eating hot foods, use a small amount. Also, don't rub your
  eyes after handling red pepper flakes.)
- 1/2 teaspoon of peeled ginger root, finely chopped
- clove of garlic, finely chopped
- 2 scallions, finely chopped

UTENSILS:

- knife
- cutting board
- large colander
- large glass or ceramic bowl
- plastic wrap
- measuring spoons

DIRECTIONS:

1. Wash cabbage leaves well. Cut into bite-sized pieces and place in colander. Add salt and mix with your hands. Let sit for 3 hours.

2. Rinse cabbage very thoroughly. Squeeze out excess liquid. Place in bowl.

3. Mix in remaining ingredients. Cover with plastic wrap and let sit at room temperature overnight. Chill before serving.

KOREAN BIRTHDAYS

A KOREAN CHILD has a special birthday party before he or she is even a year old! This day, which is called Paekil, celebrates the baby's 100th day of life. The observance of Paekil began long ago when living conditions made the survival of a new born uncertain. Today, it is still celebrated. Guests bring gifts for the infant. In turn, the family hosts a feast and gives away 100 white rice cakes to friends and neighbors.

Tol is the baby's first real birthday. At Tol, a child is considered to be two years old. This is because figuring age the traditional Korean way is different from the Western way. A baby is thought to be one year old at the time of birth. Today, Koreans use the Western way as well.

At Tol, a special ceremony is held to predict the child's future. Dressed in traditional Korean clothes, the baby is seated at a table that holds a variety of objects. The first thing he or she picks up will tell something about the future. For example, a spool of thread indicates long life. Brushes and books mean the child will become a scholar. Money or rice mean wealth. An arrow or a bow used to be included to symbolize a military career.

In Korea, special birthday parties are not just for the young. The sixtieth birthday, Hwan Gap, is considered a very important occasion. It signifies the completion of the Korean zodiac, a twelve-year cycle in which each year is represented by one of twelve animals: rat, ox, tiger, hare, dragon, snake, horse, sheep, monkey, rooster, dog, and boar. Those who have reached this age are considered to be honored persons. Formal language is used in their presence and traditional clothing is worn. The special generational bowing ceremony, kun chul, is performed to show respect for elders. It's like a sebae on New Year's Day. The Hwan Gap celebration may include feasting, singing, music, and the chanting of poetry.

Bowing, Korean Style

Although manners are no longer as formal as they were through most of Korea's history, bowing is still an important part of etiquette. It shows respect and politeness. When Koreans meet or leave each other, they bow at the waist just as you might shake hands. To show extra respect to an older person, a teacher, or an employer, you may bow a bit lower.

When visiting grandparents on special occasions like New Year's Day or a sixtieth birthday party, Koreans still practice a more formal bowing ceremony called kun chul. This bowing form is different for males and females. A boy kneels down and keeps his hands in front of him, palms down. He bends at the waist until his forehead touches the back of his hands and then he stands. Girls kneel with their hands placed at their sides as they bow their heads.

UNDERSTANDING KOREAN NAMES

*T*O WESTERN EARS, Korean names may seem unusual, yet Koreans often have three names just like many Americans. A Korean name consists of a surname (which we sometimes call a last name), a generational name, and a personal name. The Korean surname comes first. Kim is a surname. It is often (but not always) followed by the generational name, which is shared by all brothers in the same family. For example, Kim Young-ho and Kim Young-hwan would be brothers. This is the Korean way of marking seniority, or birth rank, among family members. The third name is a personal name chosen together by parents and grandparents. This name often has a poetic or promising meaning. For example, the Korean girl's name, Kim Young-hee means "glorious happiness."

While Korean girls are not always given generational names, it is interesting to note that in Korea a married woman keeps her maiden name rather than using her husband's last name.

김 영 호

김 영 환

김 영 희

KOREAN FOLKTALES
THE TIGER AND THE DRIED PERSIMMON

The Koreans tell many tales about their legendary tiger. Here is one of them:

One evening, the tiger awoke from his nap feeling especially hungry. So he decided to come down from the mountain to seek a meal in the village below. The very first farmhouse he came to had a cowshed attached. Right away, the tiger began to drool. He knew what a cowshed meant—a fat, juicy ox.

The tiger crept up to the doorway and looked inside. His dinner was sleeping peacefully. He was just getting ready to try a bite, when suddenly he heard a piercing cry!

The tiger ran outside the shed before the ox awoke and hid beneath one of the farmhouse windows. A second blood-curdling howl came trumpeting through the walls. Cautiously, the tiger peeked inside. There he saw a mother trying to quiet her baby.

"Shhh!" the mother hissed. "You'll wake up Grandmother."

But the baby only screeched louder.

"Shhh!" the mother begged. "There's a big snake outside!"

But the baby only screeched louder.

"Shhh!" the mother pleaded. "There's a big, big tiger outside!"

"What an amazing creature!" thought the tiger. "This woman knows I'm here without even seeing me."

And the baby still screeched louder.

"What fearless creatures these humans are!" marveled the tiger. "Not even their tiniest babies are afraid of me."

"You must stop crying now!" exclaimed the poor mother. "I will get a persimmon to quiet you."

To the tiger's amazement, the baby didn't utter another peep.

"What a fearsome creature a persimmon must be!" thought the tiger. "If there's one around here, perhaps it is time for me to be getting home."

Quickly, the tiger made his way back up the mountain. Inside the farmhouse, the baby sucked happily on a tasty, dried persimmon.

THE SUN AND THE MOON

*T*HIS FOLKTALE explains how the sun and the moon and came to be. Once again, it features a tiger. Can you find the part that is like Little Red Riding Hood?

A poor, widowed mother was returning home from her job on a neighboring farm when a hungry tiger came along.

"Please don't eat me!" pleaded the woman. "I have two children, a boy and a girl, who need me. Here, you can have the barley cakes I was bringing home for them in this basket."

A hungry tiger has an enormous appetite. He took the basket and ate the food. Then he ate the mother. But he was still hungry. "I will eat the woman's children, too," he decided. So he put on her clothes and hurried to her cottage.

"Who is there?" the children asked when they heard a knocking at the door.

"It is your mother," replied the tiger.

"Your voice is too gruff to be Mother's," the boy said without opening the door.

"That is from shouting to chase the birds away from the barley I have been drying," the tiger said, trying to speak more softly. "Open the door a crack so you can see my clothes."

When the children obeyed, the tiger slipped his arm inside to display the garment.

"Our mother's hand is not so hairy," the girl protested.

"You are fooled by the darkness," the tiger replied. "I am so tired from my work, children. Please let me in."

The children took pity and opened the door, and the tiger entered wearing their mother's clothing. But he had forgotten to cover his tail. Before he could catch them, the children ran outside and climbed the tree that hung over the well.

The tiger searched the yard for them. Finally, he looked in the well. He saw their reflection and thought they were inside.

"Now I will get you!" he cried. And he would have jumped in the well and drowned if the children had not giggled. The tiger looked up and saw them. Trying to hide his anger, he said in his sweetest voice, "How did you climb up so high, children?"

"We covered ourselves in cooking oil," replied the little sister. "You should, too. You will find some in the kitchen."

The tiger ran into the house and did what the little girl said. But when he came out and tried to climb the tree, he slipped and fell. The children giggled again.

Now the tiger was even angrier. This time he grabbed an ax and began chopping steps in the tree. The frightened children began to pray for a rope to take them away. Just then, one fell from the sky and lifted them above the clouds.

When the tiger saw what happened, he began to pray for a rope as well. Sure enough, another rope dropped from the sky and the tiger climbed on. But he was too heavy from having eaten the barley cakes and the children's poor mother. The rope broke and the tiger fell.

The brave children stayed in the sky. The girl became the sun and the boy became the moon.

GAMES

Yoot

YOOT IS the most popular board game in Korea. It has been played by children and adults for centuries and is especially popular at New Year's. Perhaps this is because in ancient times farmers used yoot sticks to help them predict good or bad years for crops.

The object of the game is to get your team's four playing pieces around the board to "Home." But instead of rolling dice, players toss four yoot sticks, which are flat on one side and round on the other. The way the sticks land—flat or round side up—determines how many spaces they move.

MATERIALS:

- Four yoot sticks. You can make the yoot sticks out of two 6" wooden dowels that are 1" in diameter. By cutting these dowels in half lengthwise, you will then have four sticks that are round on one side and flat on the other. Or, instead of wooden dowels, you can use carrots! Select two nice fat ones and trim off the ends. Now cut the carrots in half lengthwise to make four sticks.

- Eight checkers, buttons, or other markers to be used as playing pieces: you will need four each of two colors (for example: 4 red and 4 black)

- The yoot board. A square "throwing area," 6' x 6' is marked on the floor (use a rug, straw mat, or blanket)

HOW TO THROW THE YOOT STICKS:

- Using only one hand, hold all four sticks flat side down, crossing two over two like an "X" (see picture). Toss the sticks upward, being careful to keep them within the 6' x 6' area. Sticks that land outside the area cause the team to lose a turn. The way the sticks land determine how many spaces a playing piece is moved.

1. TO   One flat side up = one space.
2. KAE   Two flat sides up = two spaces.
3. KOL   Three flat sides up = three spaces.
4. YOOT   Four flat sides up = four spaces plus the player gets to take another turn
5. MO   Four round sides up = five spaces plus the player gets to take another turn

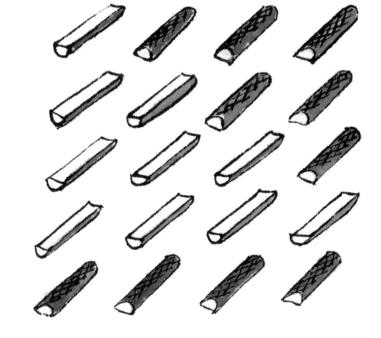

도

개

걸

윷

모

TO PLAY:

1. To determine who goes first, a player from each team tosses the yoot sticks. The team with the highest throw goes first.

2. All four playing pieces on each team begin at "Home." A player on the starting team tosses the yoot sticks and moves one piece the number of spaces indicated. Only one piece may be moved during a turn. Now a player from the opposing team takes a turn.

3. On the next round, a player may move the playing piece that is already on the board or start another.

4. A piece that lands on the same spot as one from its own team may now move together as a single unit. If a piece lands on the same spot as one from the opposing team, that piece gets sent back to "Home" to begin again.

THE BOARD:

The regular path around the board is A-B-C-D-A. Shortcuts are available to pieces that land directly on B or C. When this happens, the piece may be moved along the diagonal path through E on the next turn. The shortcuts are A-B-C-A, A-B-D-A, or the luckiest one: A-B-E-A.

Winning: The winning team is the first one to get all four playing pieces "Home."

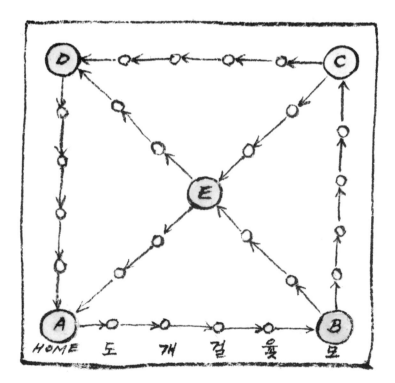

Kawi, Pawi, Po

Kawi, pawi, po means "scissors, rock, paper." Perhaps you are already familiar with this game that is played in many countries around the world, especially in Asia. It is often used before sports games as a means of deciding which person or team will go first. In Korea, kawi, pawi, po has another purpose as well. Students taking the same route home from school will often play it to decide who is going to carry everyone's book bags home. Since Korean students get plenty of homework, the loser can get stuck hauling quite a load!

To Play:
- Two players face each other and chant kawi, pawi, po. On the last word, they make one of these three signs:
- Kawi/Scissors: Index and middle finger of one hand are extended to form the blades of a scissors.
- Pawi/Rock: Clenched fist symbolizing a rock is extended.
- Po/Paper: Flat palm representing paper is extended.

Who Wins?

- Kawi (Scissors) cut paper.
- Pawi (Rock) breaks scissors.
- Po (Paper) covers rock.

Jaegi

If you enjoy playing hacky-sack, why not try your skill with a jaegi? Like quite a few other Korean games, the jaegi has been a favorite amusement for more than 2,000 years. Long ago, street vendors played to keep their feet warm during cold weather. Today, jaegi is found in schoolyards and playgrounds everywhere.

To make the jaegi, which looks like the shuttlecock in a badminton set, a Korean coin that had a hole in its center was covered with a piece of rice paper or cloth. Since that coin is no longer in circulation today, Koreans use a simple plumbing washer, which you can buy in a hardware store. Follow these steps to make a jaegi:

MATERIALS:

- one sheet of tissue paper (You can find this inside an old gift box, or at a shop that sells gift wrap.)
- steel or other metal plumbing washer, about 1" in diameter (available in any hardware store)
- scissors

DIRECTIONS:

1. Fold the sheet of tissue paper in half. Cut out a 10" x 10" square. The square will be two-layered because you have doubled the paper.
2. Place the washer at the center of the folded edge of the square. Hold the washer and the paper together and fold them over just enough to cover the washer. Now fold again and again until the paper is entirely pleated with the washer inside.
3. First, using your fingers, feel the center of the washer until you have located its hole. Carefully poke the blade of your scissors through the hole or use a pencil to poke through the tissue.
4. Pinch one end of the tissue "tail" together so you can pass it through the hole. Pull until it is snug. Next, pinch the other end of the tail together and pass it through the hole. Be patient. It will be a tight fit!
5. Fringe or feather the tail with the scissors.

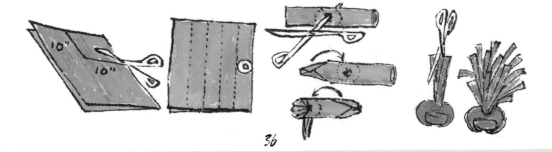

TO PLAY:

The object of the game is to keep the jaegi in the air by kicking it with the heel, toe, top, or sole of your shoe. You can keep score by counting how many times it is batted in the air before it falls to the ground. Another way to play is to kick the jaegi between two or more players until someone lets it fall. That person is eliminated and the remaining players continue until, one by one, they drop out. The winning player is the one who has not let the jaegi drop. Have fun!

LET'S EAT

IF YOU are invited for a Korean meal, you are certain to find rice and kimchi, a tangy pickled vegetable dish. These two foods, one bland but satisfying and the other sharp and spicy, are good complements to each other and to the variety of other dishes a Korean meal usually includes. Soup is served nearly as often as rice and kimchi. Fish, poultry, and beef may appear as side dishes, along with cooked and dried vegetables.

Mandu

Mandu are tasty dumplings that are often served at holiday feasts. They can be steamed, boiled, or fried.

DIRECTIONS:

INGREDIENTS FOR FRIED MANDU:

- 1/4 pound ground beef, ground sirloin, or ground round
- 1 tablespoon vegetable oil
- 1/2 medium onion, finely chopped
- 3/4 cup cabbage, shredded
- 1/2 cup small bean sprouts, chopped
- 1 scallion, finely chopped
- 1 teaspoon salt
- 1/8 teaspoon black pepper
- 30 wonton wrappers (available in Asian markets)
- 1 egg, beaten
- 1 cup vegetable oil

UTENSILS:

- cutting board
- measuring spoons and cup
- vegetable knife
- wok or large frying pan
- wooden spoon
- large bowl
- pastry brush
- kitchen towel
- tongs
- fork, teaspoon
- paper towels

1. Brown meat in frying pan, using wooden spoon to mash into little bits. Drain off fat and transfer meat to bowl.

2. Clean wok or frying pan and heat 1 tablespoon vegetable oil over high heat for one minute. Add chopped onion and adjust heat to medium. Sauté about 3 minutes until soft.

3. Toss in shredded cabbage and cook for about 3 more minutes, stirring frequently until cabbage loses crispness.

4. Now add bean sprouts and scallions. Cook about two more minutes. Remove everything from heat. Combine vegetables with meat in bowl. Add salt and pepper and mix well.

5. Place a wonton wrapper on the clean cutting board. Keep a damp towel over the rest of the package to keep wrappers moist. Dip the pastry brush lightly into the beaten egg and paint all around the edges of the wonton wrapper.

6. Place about 1 teaspoon of filling in center of wrapper. Now pick up one side and fold over to cover filling.

7. Press fork all around edges to seal dumplings. Mandu should resemble a miniature apple turnover.

8. Heat 1 cup of oil in a clean wok or frying pan over medium heat for one minute. Using tongs or chopsticks, carefully slide 5 or 6 dumplings into oil, one at a time. Fry about 3 minutes on each side. Dumplings should be golden brown. Drain on paper towels and serve.

PA JON

POPULAR PA JON are plate-size scallion pancakes. They make a tasty snack or an entire meal depending on the ingredients you choose. The dish is quick and simple to make, but ask an adult to help you with the frying.

INGREDIENTS:
- 1 cup flour
- 1 teaspoon salt
- 1 egg
- cold water
- 4 scallions, trimmed and cut into 2" matchsticks
- 2 ounces sweet red pepper, cut into 2" matchsticks
- 2 tablespoons of oil for frying

UTENSILS:
- 1/2 cup and 1 cup measuring cups
- fork
- tablespoon
- teaspoon
- large bowl
- knife
- cutting board
- 8" frying pan
- large spoon
- spatula

DIRECTIONS:
1. Put flour and salt in bowl. Crack egg into measuring cup and beat with fork. Add cold water to egg until mixture reaches the 1-cup line. Pour into bowl. Now add another 1/2 cup cold water. Mix with spoon.
2. Gently stir in matchstick scallions and red peppers.
3. Heat 1 tablespoon of oil in frying pan. Add half the batter. Let cook over medium heat for three or four minutes until golden. Turn with spatula and cook another three or four minutes.
4. Repeat with second half of batter. Each pancake can be cut into eight snack-size pieces.

There are many other ingredients you can add to your pa jon. Matchstick-size cabbage, carrot, and zucchini pieces are some good ideas but you can get as creative as you wish. Koreans also make these pancakes with shrimp and other seafood and with ground beef and other kinds of meat. If you like pa jon, experiment!

HAN'GUL, THE KOREAN ALPHABET

HAN'GUL, THE KOREAN alphabet, was invented in 1443, more than 500 years ago during the reign of King Sejong, one of Korea's greatest rulers. Before then, the Koreans used Chinese characters for their writing. But the many differences between the two languages meant the Chinese system did not always provide a way for Koreans to express what they wanted to say. Besides, for Koreans, the difficulty of learning the Chinese system was such that only the wealthiest people had the time to study and the money to hire teachers to teach them.

In order to provide his people with a system that could be learned and used by everyone, King Sejong commissioned the new alphabet. In time, poems and the Chinese classics were translated into han'gul and published for all to read. It became Korea's written language. Today, Korea has one of the highest literacy rates in the world, thanks in large part to the contribution of King Sejong.

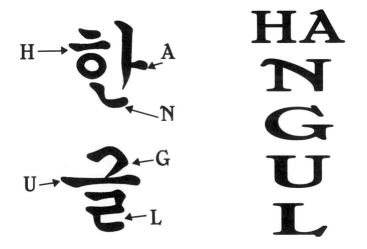

All symbols of han'gul are written from top to bottom and from left to right. Letters never appear alone, but in combinations of two, three, and sometimes four letters. The symbols on the left make the word, han'gul:

Han'gul, which is often described as a scientific alphabet, is a phonetic writing system that represents the sounds of spoken Korean. It consists of 24 letters: 14 consonants and 10 vowels. In addition, there are combinations of letters that represent 5 double consonants and 11 diphthongs. To form words or syllables, the letters are grouped in small clusters.

Here are the letters of the Korean alphabet and their sounds in English:*

CONSONANTS

HAN'GUL	ENGLISH SOUND
ㅂ	b or p
ㅊ	ch'
ㄷ	d or t
ㄱ	g or k
ㅎ	h
ㅈ	ch or j
ㅋ	k'
ㅁ	m
ㄴ	n
ㅇ	Silent before vowel or ng in middle or end of word
ㅍ	p
ㄹ	r or l
ㅅ	s (sh)
ㅌ	t'

*According to the McCune-Reischauer transcription system.

43

VOWELS

HAN'GUL	ENGLISH SOUND	
ㅏ	a (f<u>a</u>ther)	
ㅑ	ya (y<u>a</u>cht)	
ㅓ	o (<u>o</u>nion)	These vowels are written next to the consonants.
ㅕ	yo (y<u>oun</u>g)	
ㅣ	i (ma<u>ga</u>z<u>i</u>ne)	
ㅗ	o (h<u>o</u>me)	
ㅛ	yo (y<u>o</u>del)	
ㅜ	oo (sp<u>oo</u>l)	These vowels are written under the consonants.
ㅠ	yu (y<u>ou</u>)	
ㅡ	u (p<u>u</u>p)	

* According to the McCune-Reischauer transcription system.

Peter	피터	Jessica	제시카
Susan	수잔	Barbara	바바라
Mary	매리	Joanne	죠앤
Adam	아담	Helen	헬렌
Michael	마이클	Eugene	유진
James	제임스	Joyce	조이스

44

Let's Write Han'gul

Hello/Goodbye	ahn nyong	안녕
Mother	omoni	어머니
Father	aboji	아버지
School	hakkyo	학교
House	chip	집
Car	ch'a	차
Friend	ch'in'gu	친구
Tiger	horangi	호랑이

Proverbs, Sokdam

THE PROVERBS of a people tell us a lot about their values, beliefs, and culture. Some of the best-known American proverbs come from Benjamin Franklin, who published them in the mid-1700's as part of POOR RICHARD'S ALMANAC. Thrift, hard work, duty, and responsibility were all part of the principles behind these proverbs. Some examples you may have heard include: "A stitch in time saves nine"; "Early to bed, early to rise, makes a man healthy, wealthy and wise"; "A penny saved is a penny earned"; and "The early bird catches the worm."

Koreans, too, have their proverbs, which are known as sokdam. They are very old and present bits of philosophy to live by. These familiar sayings have been passed down from generation to generation of Koreans. Some of them have English equivalents that are quite well known among Americans. Perhaps you will recognize some of them.

Eat Chinese Mustard and Cry

울며 겨자 먹기

This proverb is used to mean "accept the bad along with the good." Even though hot mustard is delicious on many foods, it may bring tears to your eyes.

To Begin Is to Be Half Done

시작이 반이다

Koreans say this to mean "getting started is half the job." The next time you are facing an afternoon of homework, think of this proverb.

If You Eat a Late Breakfast, You Will Go to a Closing Market

늦은 밥 먹고 파장 간다

In many areas of Korea, outdoor markets are held once or twice a week. These open early and close shortly after noon. A Korean parent may say this to chide a child who oversleeps. It's a lot like the American expression, "The early bird catches the worm."

The Dog at a Village School Will Be Writing Poetry Within Three Years

서당개 삼 년에 풍월한다

Although today Korean students attend modern schools much like those in the West, the village schools of the past were quite different. Students learned lessons by endless chanting and repetition. The origin of this proverb probably comes from those lessons. It is meant to scold a lazy student by suggesting that even a dog could learn just by being in class.

Even a Tiger Will Appear If You Talk About Him

호랑이도 제 말하면 온다

Did you ever notice that when you criticize someone who's not around, that person usually shows up unexpectedly? This expression is about just such happenings and is similar to the English saying, "Speak of the devil!"

BIBLIOGRAPHY

The Asia Society. DISCOVER KOREA, FAMILY AND HOME. New York: The Asia Society, 1987.

The Asia Society, DISCOVER KOREA,SCHOOL AND COMMUNITY, NEW YORK:The Asia Society, 1988.

Chung, Okwha, and Monroe, Judy. COOKING THE KOREAN WAY. Minneapolis, MN: Lerner Publications Co., 1988.

Farley, Carole. KOREA, LAND OF THE MORNING CALM. Minneapolis, MN: Dillon Press, Inc., 1991.

GAMES OF THE WORLD. Geneva: Swiss Committee for UNICEF, 1975.

Grant, Bruce K. KOREAN PROVERBS, DRAGON HEAD, SNAKE TAIL, and A FROG IN A WELL. Seoul, Korea: Wu Ah Dang, 1982.

Haskins, Jim. COUNT YOUR WAY THROUGH KOREA. Minneapolis, MN: Carolrhoda Books, Inc., 1989.

KOREAN ARTS AND CULTURE. Seoul, Korea: Seoul International Publishing House, 1986.

Lee, Jung Young. SOKDAM, CAPSULES OF KOREAN WISDOM. Seoul, Korea: Seoul Computer Press, 1983.

Marks, Copeland with Kim, Manjo. THE KOREAN KITCHEN. San Francisco: Chronicle Books, 1993.

Setton, Mark C.K., THE SUN AND THE MOON. Seoul, Korea: Si-Sa-Yong-O-Sa, Inc., 1985.